Let's Draw
Dinosaurs

Author
Susie Hodge

Artist
Steve Roberts

WINDMILL
BOOKS ™

New York

Published in 2011 by Windmill Books, LLC
303 Park Avenue South, Suite #1280, New York, NY 10010-3657

Adaptations to North American Edition © 2011 Windmill Books, LLC
Copyright © 2011 Miles Kelly Publishing

Library of Congress Cataloging-in-Publication Data

Hodge, Susie, 1960–
Dinosaurs / by Susie Hodge ; illustrated by Steve Roberts.
       p. cm. — (Let's draw)
       Includes index.
       ISBN 978-1-61533-264-9 (library binding) —
ISBN 978-1-61533-267-0 (pbk.) — ISBN 978-1-61533-290-8 (6-pack)
1. Dinosaurs in art—Juvenile literature. 2. Drawing—Technique—Juvenile
       literature. I. Roberts, Steve. II. Title.
                 NC780.5.H59 2011
                 743.6—dc22
                                          2010042196

Manufactured in the United States of America

CPSIA Compliance Information: Batch #BW2011WM: For Further Information contact Windmill Books,
New York, New York at 1-866-478-0556

contents

Materials

ALL YOU NEED TO START DRAWING IS A PENCIL AND SOME PAPER. IF YOU COLLECT SOME OTHER MATERIALS, THOUGH, YOU WILL BE ABLE TO CREATE EVEN MORE EXCITING EFFECTS IN YOUR DRAWINGS.

Crayons
Wax crayons can be used on their own or with other materials to produce lots of interesting results.

Colored pencils
The simplest way to add color is with colored pencils. Some can be blended with water to turn them into watercolors. You can also layer colored pencils on top of each other to make new colors.

Pencils
Soft pencils make black, smudgy lines. Hard pencils make light, thin lines.

Hard pencil

Soft pencil

Paper
Try using different types of papers such as heavy drawing paper, tissue paper, and construction paper to add extra texture to your drawings.

corrugated paper adds extra depth to bumpy textures.

Charcoal and chalk

Charcoal comes in black, brittle sticks. These can be smudged and blended easily to create shadowy, dramatic pictures. Chalk pastels are good for adding highlights, and are best used on colored paper.

Felt-tip pens

Pens can be used to add a more cartoonish feel to your drawings. You can use them to define outlines and create dramatic patterns and markings.

Other equipment

Firm erasers will get rid of most pencil and some colored pencil marks. Kneaded erasers can be squashed into all sorts of shapes to "lift" marks off the page. A good pencil sharpener is useful. Use paintbrushes to add water to water-soluble colored pencils.

Buy handmade paper from gift or art stores.

Textured paper makes an excellent background.

shading

To MAKE YOUR DINOSAURS LOOK THREE DIMENSIONAL, YOU'LL NEED TO ADD DARK SHADING AND WHITE HIGHLIGHTS TO YOUR DRAWINGS. THESE ARE CALLED TONES.

When the light source is above the dinosaur, its back is palest.

Light and dark
In bright light, tones are strong and defined. In dull light, tones are less contrasting. Dark tones always fall in places the light doesn't touch.

Pale blue is used for the lightest areas.

Dark purple gives the neck shading and shape.

Using color
You can add shading using black. You can also try using other dark colors, such as dark blue or brown. Highlights can be created using white or by leaving areas of the paper blank. You can also use any pale shade that contrasts with the main body, such as yellow and pale blue.

Brown is used for the dark areas.

Highlights

To give your drawings depth, add highlights to areas of deep colors so that they contrast brightly. You can create highlights by leaving areas of white paper empty or coloring over with white pastel or colored pencil.

Leaving pale patches in dark-colored areas makes the surface look shiny.

Hatching

Draw thick lines close together to create dark tones, and farther apart to make light tones.

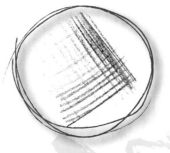

Cross-hatching

For darker shading, draw hatching lines that cross each other. Closer lines make darker tones.

Stippling

Draw dots close together for dark tones and farther apart for lighter tones.

Triple tone

To create delicate shading that looks realistic, your areas of shadow should progress from light to dark gradually. Go over the darkest areas again, pressing harder, and then press more gently as you reach the medium areas to blend light and dark.

Shading goes gradually from light to dark.

Texture

TEXTURE IS THE WAY SOMETHING FEELS WHEN IT IS TOUCHED. DINOSAURS WERE REPTILES, SO MOST OF THEM PROBABLY HAD BUMPY, SCALY SKIN. HERE'S HOW YOU CAN CREATE TEXTURE IN YOUR DRAWINGS.

Scales and wrinkles

To make the textures you draw on your dinosaurs look realistic, don't draw every single scale or bump. Add lots of detail on the parts of the dinosaur that are nearest, and more sketchy detail on the parts that are farthest away.

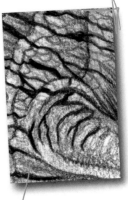

Scales

Add overlapping circular pencil marks over white paper or a base color.

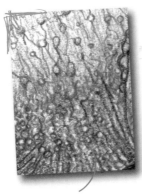

Feathers

Draw lots of tiny lines, all going in the same direction.

Bumps

Use a sharpened pencil to draw thin wavy lines and small circles.

Wrinkles

Draw your base colors, then use a black pencil to create thick lines that crisscross one another.

Patterned skin
It is thought that many dinosaurs had markings on their skin to help them blend into their surroundings.

Spots
Use two colors to make the base color. Then use darker versions of both colors to draw lines of shadow over the top.

DRAW TEXTURES IN THE DIRECTIONS THEY GROW OR APPEAR AND MAKE THEM DARKER IN DARK-TONED AREAS. NEVER TRY TO DRAW ALL THE TEXTURES YOU SEE. LEAVE THE HIGHLIGHTED AREAS WITHOUT ANY MARKS.

Stripes
Bold, scribbly stripes in a color that contrasts with the main body color look dramatic.

Perspective

OBJECTS SEEM SMALLER TO THE VIEWER THE FARTHER AWAY THEY ARE. THIS MEANS THAT AN OBJECT IN THE FOREGROUND OF A DRAWING SHOULD APPEAR BIGGER THAN AN OBJECT IN THE BACKGROUND. THIS IS CALLED PERSPECTIVE.

Color

Use bright colors on the areas of your subject closest to the viewer. Use paler colors on the parts that are farther away to create the impression of distance.

From the side, Polacanthus' head looks small, but its body is huge.

Foreshortening

When drawing a dinosaur walking toward you, the parts that are closest, such as the head, will seem much bigger than they really are compared to the rest of the body. This is called foreshortening.

From the front, the head and front legs look much bigger.

Action

SOME DINOSAURS WERE FAST HUNTERS, WHILE OTHERS SLOWLY WALKED THE EARTH. HERE'S SOME IDEAS TO GET ALL KINDS OF DINOSAURS MOVING.

Movement lines show that Spinosaurus is whipping its tail quickly back and forth.

Once you have drawn your dinosaur, try smudging chalk pastels around the outline or drawing broken lines to give the idea of movement.

To draw a heavy, lumbering dinosaur, make the tones closest to the ground as dark as you can. This helps to make the dinosaur look heavy.

Brachiosaurus

1 Draw a large oval body. Draw four thick legs, a long neck, and a small, round head.

The head is a tiny circle compared to the body.

Draw a curving "J" shape for a tail.

2 Shape the legs and neck using curving lines. Add the snout and the eye.

Curve the neck.

Thicken the tail to fit on the oval body.

3 To show tone, lightly hatch small lines where the light does not reach.

Add a crest to the head and draw the open mouth.

Don't forget the toenails.

4 Add color using soft blues and grays. Make the skin look textured by drawing rough horizontal strokes over the base color.

Shadowy areas are dark, with highlights of reddish-pink.

Try working on dark paper. Draw shadows in black and dark purple and highlights in white and pale blue.

Allosaurus

1 Draw the body and legs as a collection of triangles. Add a curving tail.

The leg in the back is smaller than the leg in front.

2 Add curves around the outside of your guidelines. The curve at the back of the head is similar to the curve of the back.

3 Erase the guidelines. Add details such as the claws, mouth, eye, and the ridges on top of the snout.

4 Show tone and texture using light pencil marks, leaving the paper white where the light is shining.

5 Color your drawing using green, then add orange to highlight. Use slightly rough markings on the body to show the scaly texture of the skin.

Try drawing on textured paper. Use dull pencils to create a base color. Then use a brown pencil to add circular shapes and squiggly lines on top.

ornithomimus

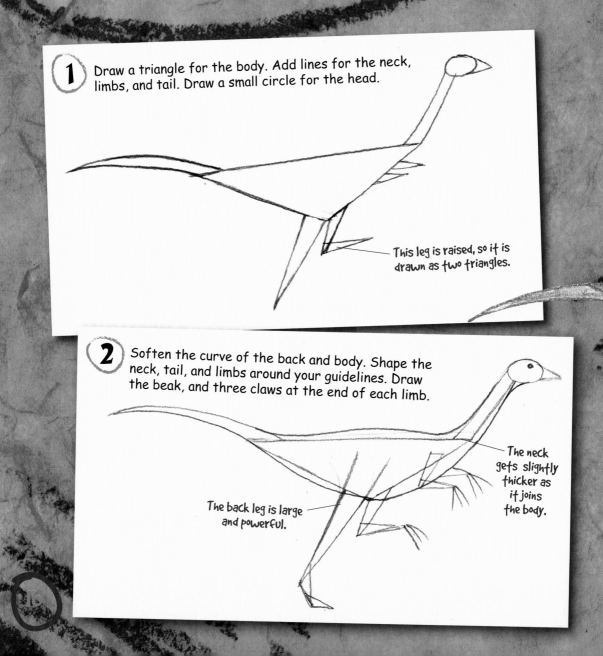

1 Draw a triangle for the body. Add lines for the neck, limbs, and tail. Draw a small circle for the head.

This leg is raised, so it is drawn as two triangles.

2 Soften the curve of the back and body. Shape the neck, tail, and limbs around your guidelines. Draw the beak, and three claws at the end of each limb.

The neck gets slightly thicker as it joins the body.

The back leg is large and powerful.

3 Show texture by drawing lines to show the muscles on the neck, body, and tail. Shade the darker areas and add detail to the features.

Shape the legs.

4 Blend colors, working from dark blue on the back to yellow for the belly. Use your pencil to add a few circular scales and spots.

Triceratops

1 Draw an oval that ends in a point at one end. Add four legs and a curving tail.

The neck frill starts as a semicircle.

2 Add the horns. Begin to shape the head by drawing the beaklike mouth.

3 Start to shade in the tones and wrinkles under and around the legs. Shape the head and the neck frill.

Draw the eye.

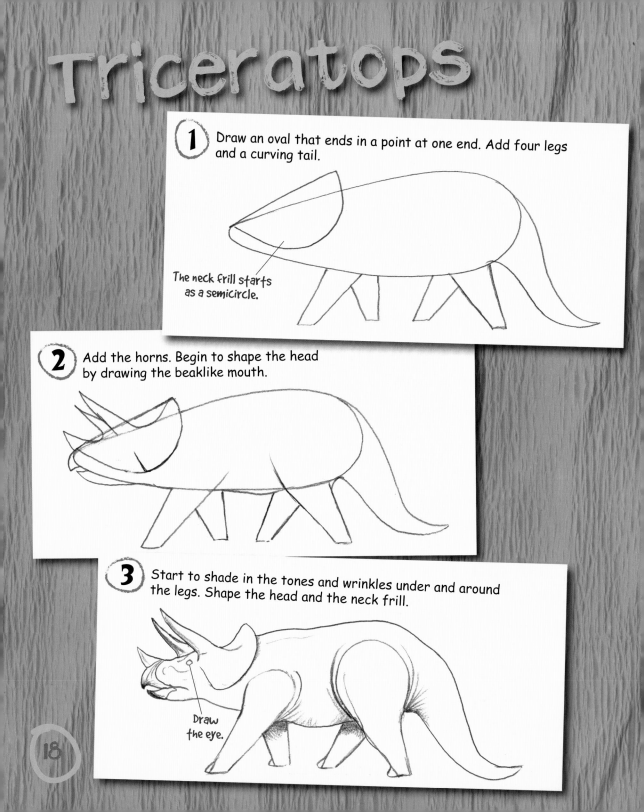

4 Shade the horns. Add detail to the head and skin.

5 Add color using greens and blues. Use brown for details and shadows. Leave some pale highlights on the horns and around the mouth.

Create bumpy skin by drawing circles in greens and browns. Then use a sharp pencil to draw lines, following the outlines of parts of the circles.

Ankylosaurus

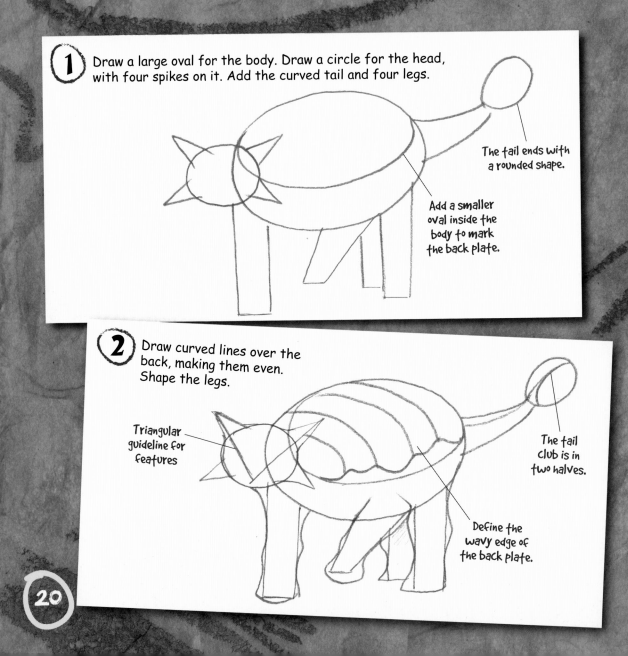

1 Draw a large oval for the body. Draw a circle for the head, with four spikes on it. Add the curved tail and four legs.

The tail ends with a rounded shape.

Add a smaller oval inside the body to mark the back plate.

2 Draw curved lines over the back, making them even. Shape the legs.

Triangular guideline for features

The tail club is in two halves.

Define the wavy edge of the back plate.

3 Add rows of spikes on the back plate. Draw the detail on the head and shade the body and legs.

The spikes that are farthest away are smallest.

Short stubby claws

4 Make the body orange and the back plate blue. The spikes are bone-colored with brown shadows.

Color in small circles, pressing hard to create the rough texture.

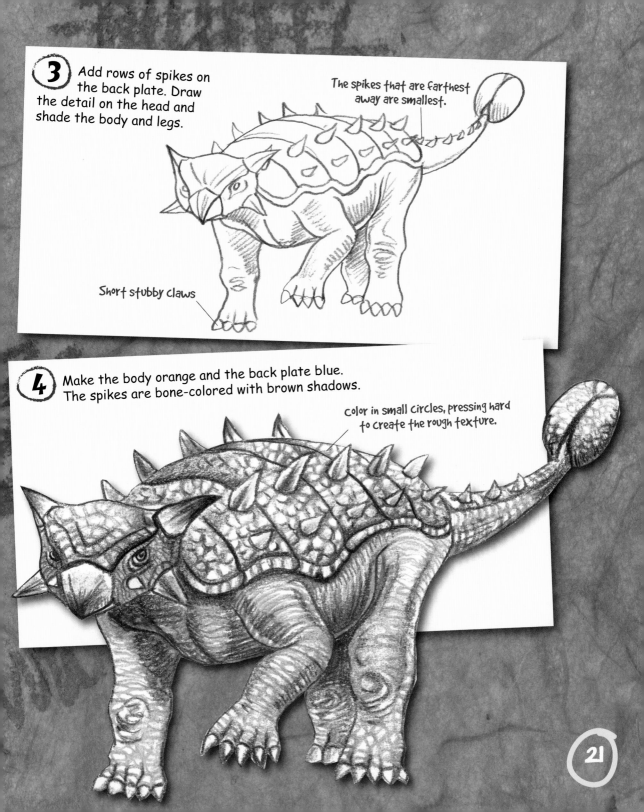

velociraptor

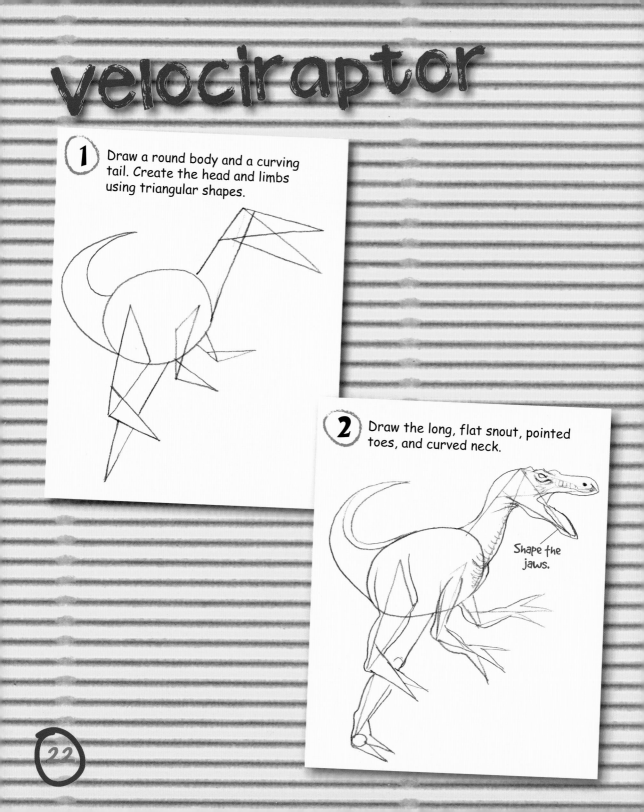

1 Draw a round body and a curving tail. Create the head and limbs using triangular shapes.

2 Draw the long, flat snout, pointed toes, and curved neck.

Shape the jaws.

3 Erase the guidelines. Add detail and tone with soft lines. Draw the teeth and claws.

Darken features.

This line adds perspective to the tail.

Try using watercolor pencils to color in the markings. Then wet a thin brush and go over your colors gently, blending them slightly.

4 Color your drawing, following the markings you have sketched. Make your shading paler on the head.

spinosaurus

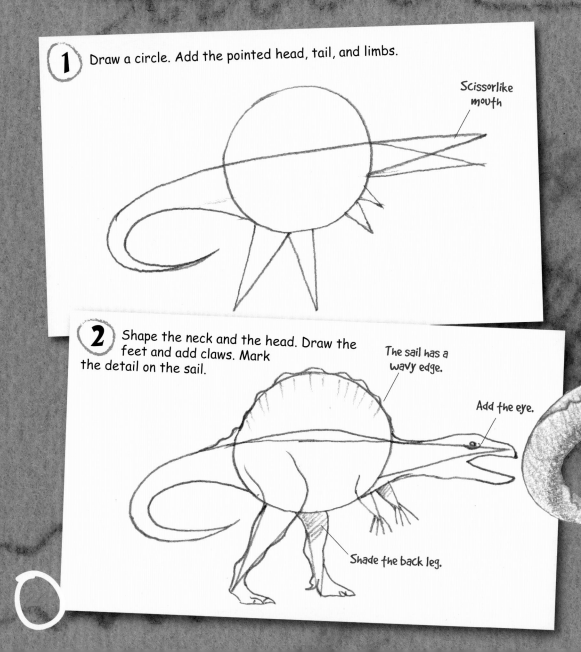

1 Draw a circle. Add the pointed head, tail, and limbs.

Scissorlike mouth

2 Shape the neck and the head. Draw the feet and add claws. Mark the detail on the sail.

The sail has a wavy edge.

Add the eye.

Shade the back leg.

3 Draw the patterned skin using soft pencil marks. Erase the guidelines and shape the head.

4 Add color using purple and red, following your markings. Add highlights in pale orange.

compsognathus

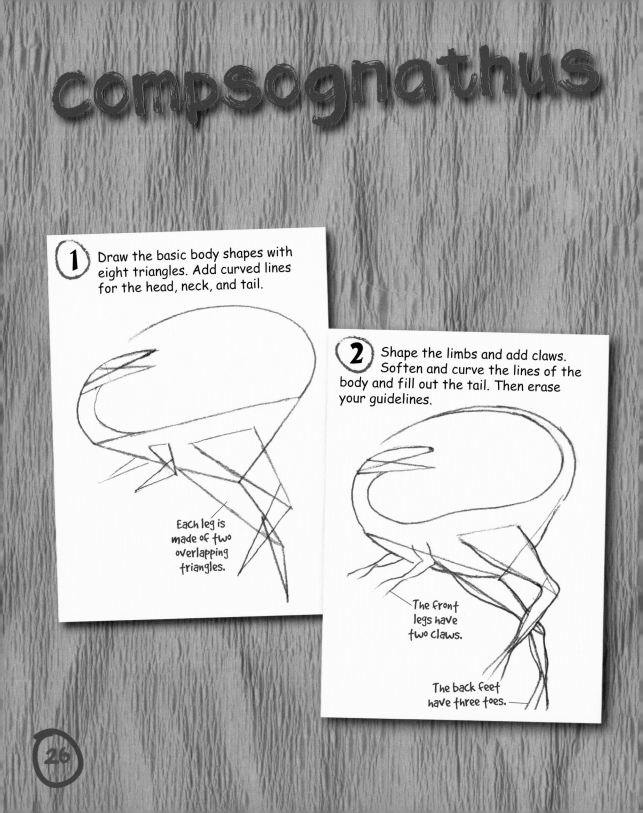

1 Draw the basic body shapes with eight triangles. Add curved lines for the head, neck, and tail.

Each leg is made of two overlapping triangles.

2 Shape the limbs and add claws. Soften and curve the lines of the body and fill out the tail. Then erase your guidelines.

The front legs have two claws.

The back feet have three toes.

3 Add shading with hatched lines. Show feathers by using short lines to blur the outline of the back, head, and tail.

Add detail to the head.

Shade the back leg.

4 Add texture by using lots of short strokes, all going in the same direction.

To achieve a feathery texture draw short, soft pencil lines in different colors all going the same way. Then use a very sharp pencil to add tiny lines to some feathers.

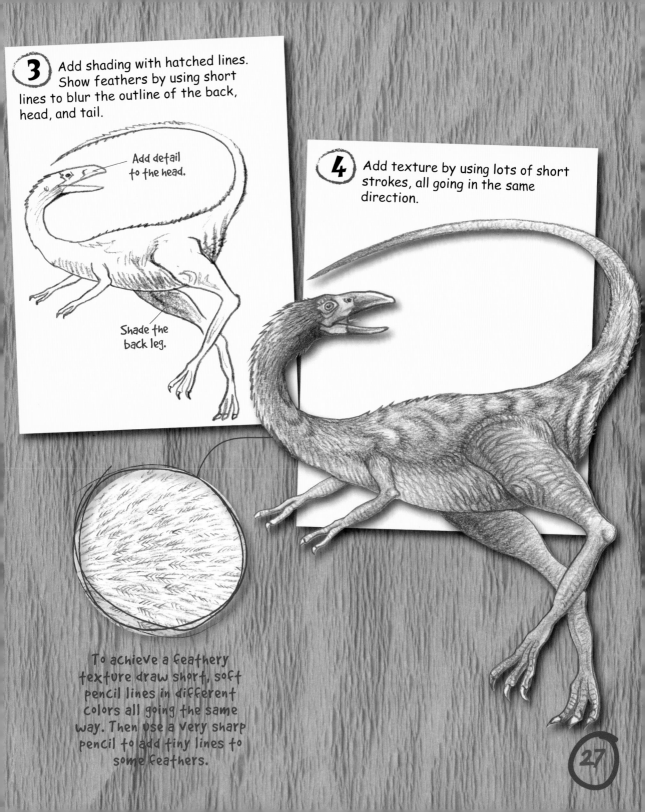

stegosaurus

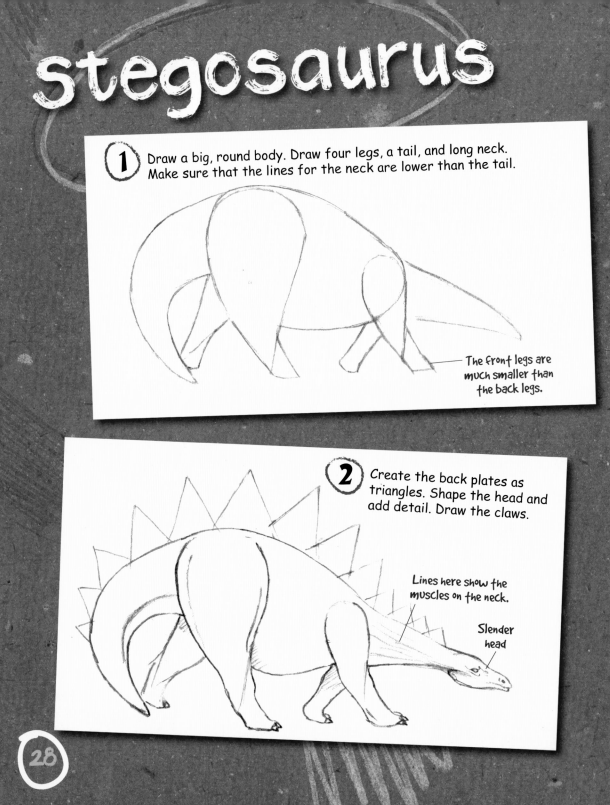

1 Draw a big, round body. Draw four legs, a tail, and long neck. Make sure that the lines for the neck are lower than the tail.

The front legs are much smaller than the back legs.

2 Create the back plates as triangles. Shape the head and add detail. Draw the claws.

Lines here show the muscles on the neck.

Slender head

3 Shape the plates along the back and tail. Draw four spikes on the end of the tail.

4 Use shading and color to make the skin look scaly. Use blue and green on the top of the body, and yellow and red for the plates and belly. Layer dark blue over green with touches of black in the darkest places.

Try drawing your dinosaur on pale green paper. Then create the look of textured skin by drawing wiggly lines in blue, dark green, and orange over the top.

Tyrannosaurus

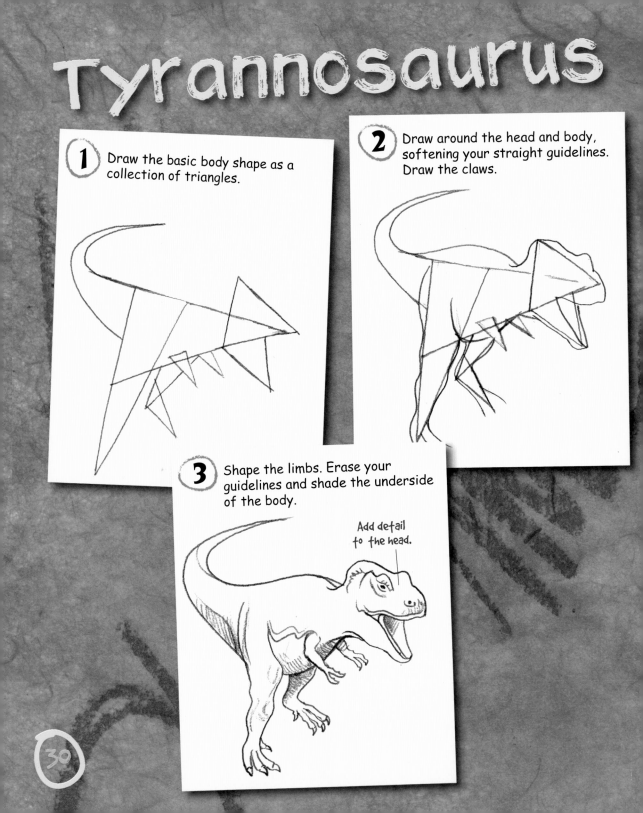

1 Draw the basic body shape as a collection of triangles.

2 Draw around the head and body, softening your straight guidelines. Draw the claws.

3 Shape the limbs. Erase your guidelines and shade the underside of the body.

Add detail to the head.